INTRODUCTION

The introduction of the National Curriculum focussed attention on spelling. Testing at 7, 11, 14 and 16 has been a much debated issue, but it is clear that from the evidence of Key Stage 1 tests and remarks from G.C.S.E. examiners that spelling is an area that needs to be addressed by both primary and secondary schools.

Spelling has always been controversial. On the one hand there is the view that a child's writing is sacred and not to be defaced by the red pen at any cost. On the other, one finds the teaching group that seizes upon every spelling mistake, no matter how understandable or creative.

What is not in doubt, is that at G.C.S.E. examination level the decision has been taken to penalize pupils who produce poor spelling. Needless-to-say, this could make a significant difference to a pupil's final grade and not surprisingly many parents are asking what secondary schools are doing about spelling.

The production of a whole school approach to spelling is a matter for individual schools and not a topic for discussion in this spelling resource material. However, it is the authors' belief that a cohesive approach to marking and a clear policy on spelling will enhance a pupil's mastery of this very important skill. With this in mind, the Folens photocopiable material offers a range of spelling activities specifically designed for pupils in the Key Stage 3 phase at secondary school who are experiencing difficulties with spelling.

Many secondary school pupils will require help not only with the specific subject vocabulary, but also the 'bread and butter' words like - was, they, said, because ...etc.

This resource provides a bank of photocopiable material to meet both these needs and enables all pupils to benefit from a systematic approach to spelling. The resource also includes several pages with pre-drawn graphics, but left blank for the teacher to write in words so that the material can be 'tailored' specifically for individual pupils.

THE SPELLING STRATEGY

Teachers use various approaches to promote the teaching of spelling, including copying out a spelling mistake a number of times, teaching and testing ten spellings a week, etc.

Whatever the policy adopted by individual schools we believe it is important to promote a strategy which embraces the philosophy of LOOK, SAY, COVER, WRITE and CHECK.

LOOK

Spelling has a strong visual element. The pupils should be encouraged to study the construction of individual words. Attention should be drawn to the fact that words are not a series of unrelated letters, but are made up of regularly recurring letter patterns such as: 'ain' in the following words: pain, paint, rain, sprain, strain, again or 'ent' in present, parent, sent, spent, different. Drawing attention to the important letter pattern by using a highlighter pen or by underlining can help pupils memorise the important structure of the word.

SAY

Good spelling also has a spoken element. Correct articulation of words may often help. So too, does the ability to listen carefully to how a word is pronounced.

COVER

Spelling is a skill that requires pupils to write words from memory, therefore, it is important to encourage children to memorise the visual image of words. Simply copying words has a limited impact. Therefore, it is necessary to ensure that pupils cover the words before they try to spell them. Once the word is covered the child is dependent on visual memory in order to recall and write them. The skill of memorising a word needs encouragement and practice. Teaching the Look, Say, Cover, Write and Check strategy will help provide this.

WRITE

Having covered the word the pupil should then be asked to write the word without copying. The use of letter patterns and the reinforcement of the 'feel' of writing helps the spelling of words. With practice, the letter pattern itself takes on the form of a single unit which just flows from the writer's pen without too much thought.

CHECK

Once the word has been written the pupils should always be encouraged to cross check their spelling of the word with the original. If it is correct they should be congratulated. Where it is wrong they should be encouraged to identify the part of the word they mis-spelt and to concentrate on putting that part right by repeating the procedure of Look, Say, Cover, Write and Check.

USING THE SHEETS

The sheets may be used by different teachers:
- by the Special Needs teacher
- by the English Department
- by other subject departments

Within these settings they may be used:
- with the whole class
- with groups
- with specific individuals as appropriate

The sheets may be used:
- as a basis for specific lessons
- as part of a lesson (e.g., after identifying a particular spelling difficulty)
- as homework assignments

The sheets may be used:
- independently by the pupils
- with teacher support (Their effectiveness is obviously enhanced by teacher involvement and discussion.)

Features of the sheets (These features are common to most of the sheets)

Key to Spelling

Most sheets have a 'Key to Spelling' flash which emphasises and reinforces the main point of the sheet. Draw the pupil's attention to this at the beginning of each assignment and again at the end as part of the review process.

School context and use of the 'teacher' visual

Using comic characters provides plenty of humour and opportunities for discussion. The 'teacher' visuals towards the top of the pages explain spelling points being made and give instructions for working the assignments.

The assignments

These usually consist of some form of spelling activity which involves learning ten or so words embodying a particular spelling point. These may be worked independently or, if appropriate, with a partner.

After completing the assignments the box at the bottom of each page encourages pupils to check their spellings. It is suggested that this should be done either by a partner or by the teacher, to ensure they are correct.

The pupils are then asked to turn over, and on the blank side of their sheets, use the LOOK, SAY, COVER, WRITE, CHECK spelling strategy to learn these words.

The spinner and cubes on pages 46 and 47 have been left blank so teachers can personalise these for pupils with individual spelling problems.

Assessment

After practising the words, using the spelling strategy, and when they feel fairly confident, it is suggested that the pupils get a partner (or the teacher) to test them.

The 'Spellometer' provides a good method of recording results. It provides a cumulative record of spelling progress and is a visual incentive to try to maintain progress and improvement.

A self-assessment sheet 'My Spelling Hit List' provides a means of responding to concerns raised by individual pupils.

Spelling

LOUIS FIDGE
PHILIP BELL

Folens
COPYMASTER

CONTENTS

Louis Fidge and Philip Bell hereby assert their moral rights to be identified as the authors of this work in accordance with the Copyright, Designs and Patents Act 1988.

Illustrations: Eric Jones   Cover design: Abacus Art
Cover image: Peter Ryan

© 1992 Folens Limited, on behalf of the authors.
Reprinted 1997.

First published 1992 by Folens Limited, Dunstable and Dublin.
Folens Limited, Albert House, Apex Business Centre, Boscombe Road, Dunstable, LU5 4RL, United Kingdom.

ISBN 1 85276 297-7

Printed in Singapore by Craft Print.

KEY TO SPELLING — CRACKING THE CODE

Look for common letter patterns in words.

MUSEUM EGYPTOLOGY GALLERY

Use this code to help you write the words below.

A	B	C	D	E	F	G	H	I	J	K	L	M	N	O

P	O	R	S	T	U	V	W	X	Y	Z

CHALLENGE!

Write some words for your partner in code.

BOARD

CLOAK

ROAD

COAST

FOAM

GOAL

SOAK

GROAN

BOAST

THROAT

How I got on

10	**Hot shot speller**
9	
8	
7	**Need some more practice**
6	
5	
4	
3	
2	**Need lots of practice**
1	
0	

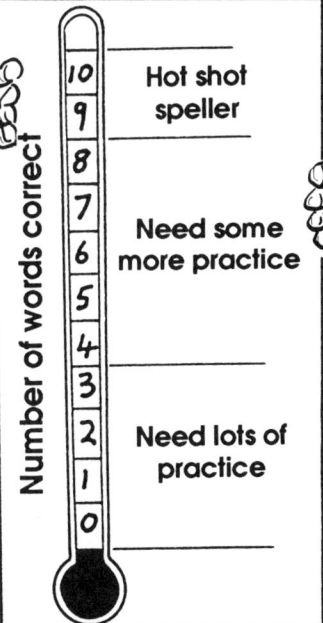

Number of words correct

THE SPELLOMETER

NOW Get someone to check your spellings. Turn over and try to write the words correctly several times without copying. Then get a partner to test you.

FAIR EXCHANGE

Nearly every word has at least one vowel sound in it.

I'LL GIVE YOU THIS FOR A GO ON YOUR GAME.

MOOoo
TWEET TWEET
PING PING
BAAA

FAIR ENOUGH.

MEGA POP

20,000 No. 1s ON THIS

Exchange the numbers in the words below for vowels.

1 ↔ a	2 ↔ e	3 ↔ i	4 ↔ o	5 ↔ u

Now write the word without copying.

Make up some more examples like these for a partner to try.

b 2 c 1 5 s 2

1 l r 2 1 dy

br 4 5 ght

2 n 4 5 g h

fr 3 2 n d

g 5 2 s s

n 1 5 ghty

l 4 n 2 l y

4 n c 2

br 4 k 2 n

How I got on

Number of words correct

10 — Hot shot speller
9
8
7
6 — Need some more practice
5
4
3
2 — Need lots of practice
1
0

THE SPELLOMETER

NOW

Get someone to check your spellings. Turn over and try to write the words correctly several times without copying. Then get a partner to test you.

IN—A—SPIN

- Stick the hexagon shapes on to card.

- Cut them out.

- Push a (cocktail) stick through the centre of each to make them into spinners.

- Spin them both and see how many different words you can make.

- Keep a note of all the words.

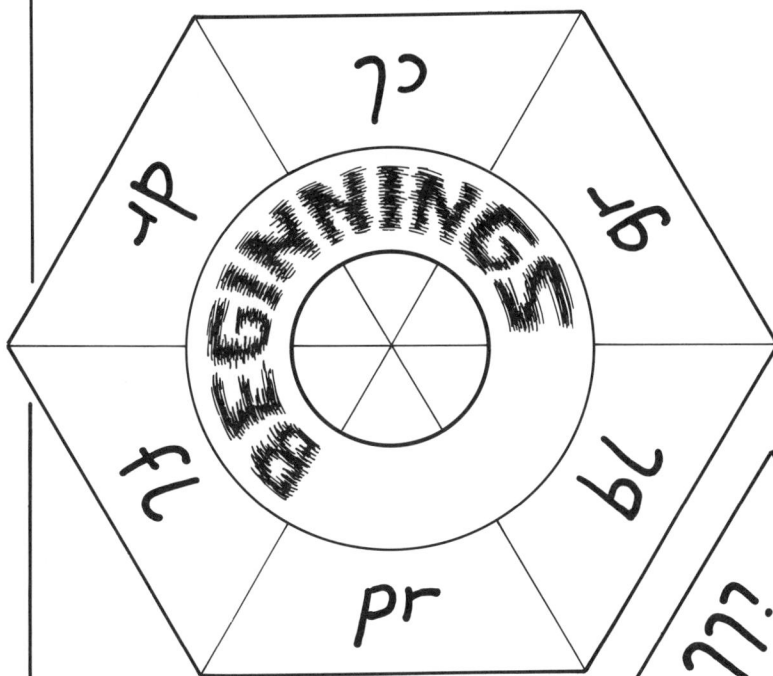

BEGINNINGS

cr
gr
br
pr
fl
dr

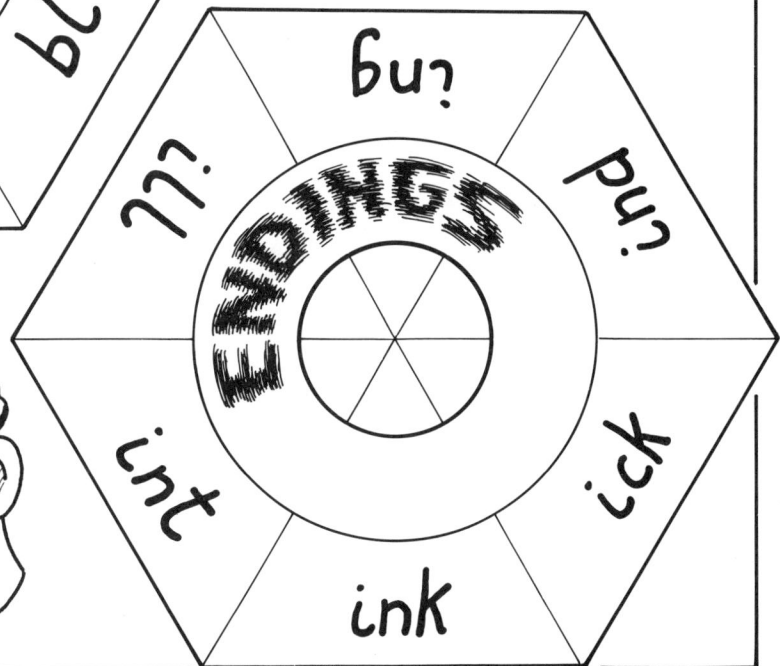

ENDINGS

ing
und
ick
ink
int
ill

This page may be photocopied for classroom use only

Although words may have similar letter patterns they don't always sound the same.

THROWING IN THE TOWEL!

OW

SHOWERS

Write the missing 'ow' letter pattern on each towel – then write the whole word on the blank towel next to it.

Say each word. Does the 'ow' always make the same sound?

t_el		h_	
n_		d_n	
l_		elb_	
p_der		sh_er	
shad_		fl_er	

How I got on

Number of words correct

10	Hot shot speller
9	
8	
7	
6	Need some more practice
5	
4	
3	
2	Need lots of practice
1	
0	

THE SPELLOMETER

NOW

Get someone to check your spellings. Turn over. Practise spelling these 10 words without copying. Get a partner to test you.

KEY TO SPELLING

MIXING WORDS

Sometimes we can join two words together and make a longer word.

hand → writing → handwriting

Have a go at mixing the words below together to make new words.

after	how	
some	self	
any	noon	afternoon
out	ever	
my	one	
under	side	
when	table	
down	where	
time	stand	
every	stairs	

How I got on

Number of words correct

10	Hot shot speller
9	
8	
7	
6	Need some more practice
5	
4	
3	
2	Need lots of practice
1	
0	

THE SPELLOMETER

NOW Get someone to check your spellings. Turn over. Practise spelling the 10 new words you have mixed together without copying. Get a partner to test you.

TOOLS OF THE TRADE

Write down all the small words you can find in the name of each tool.

Look for small words inside longer words.

Learning in the Laboratory

HOW MANY SMALL WORDS CAN YOU SEE INSIDE THIS LONG WORD?

LABORATORY

CHALLENGE!

Look carefully at the word on the board. Say it to yourself slowly. Cover it. Try to write it without copying!

Look at the words below. Say them. Circle any small words you can find in each. Write the longer words without copying!

rat

bat

flat

what

water

for

form

cork

torch

work

How I got on

Number of words correct	
10	Hot shot speller
9	
8	
7	Need some more practice
6	
5	
4	
3	
2	Need lots of practice
1	
0	

THE SPELLOMETER

NOW Turn over and try to write the words correctly several times without copying. Then get a partner to test you.

Look out for words that double the last letter when you add 'ing'.

COME ON! YOU CAN RUN FASTER THAN THAT!

I'M RUNNING AS FAST AS I CAN!

WARNING!

We can just add 'ing' to lots of verbs without changing them.

catch + ing ⟶ catching

BUT if the next to last letter is a vowel we sometimes double the last letter then add 'ing'

run + ing ⟶ running

Make the verbs below into 'ing' words - but be careful!

bat ⟶

bend ⟶

crawl ⟶

drop ⟶

hit ⟶

hop ⟶

jump ⟶

sit ⟶

swim ⟶

stand ⟶

NOW

Get someone to check the spellings of your 'ing' words. Practise spelling them on the back of this sheet without copying. Get a partner to help you.

How I got on

Number of words correct

10 9 8 — Hot shot speller

7 6 5 — Need some more practice

4 3 2 1 0 — Need lots of practice

THE SPELLOMETER

- Stick the hexagon shapes on to card.

- Cut them out.

- Push a (cocktail) stick through the centre of each to make them into spinners.

- Spin them both and see how many different words you can make.

- Keep a note of all the words.

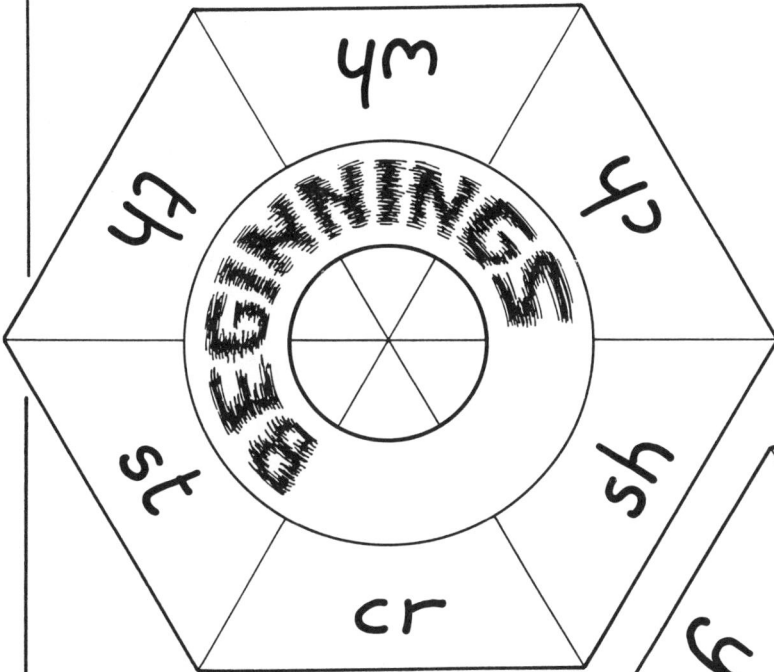

BEGINNINGS

ym · yp · sh · cr · st · fl

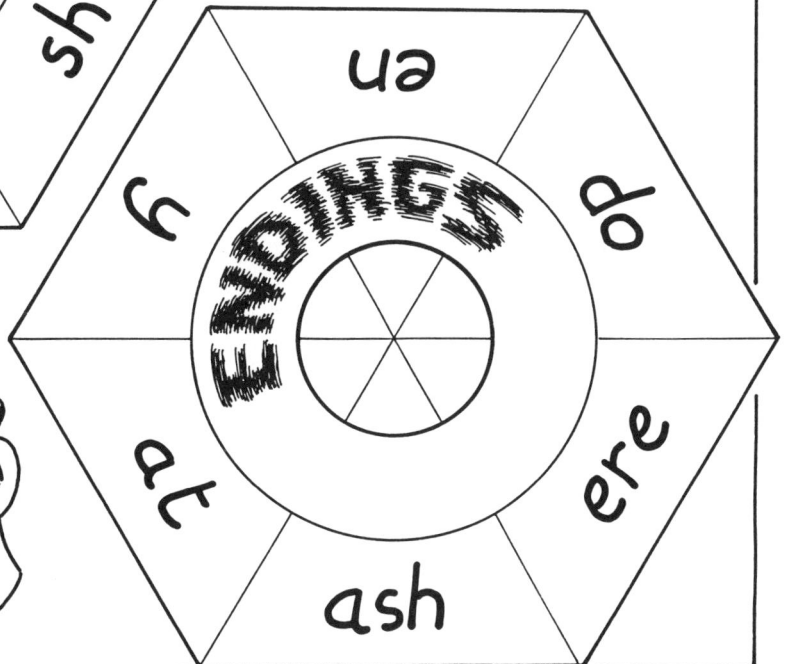

ENDINGS

ua · do · ere · ash · at · g

This page may be photocopied for classroom use only

KEY TO SPELLING — CHANGING WORDS

Adding an 'e' to the end of a short word often changes its meaning.

I LIKE THIS CAP AND CAPE.

I HATE THIS HAT.

DRAMA PROPS BOX

cap + e → cape

hat + e → hate

When we wear different clothes it changes us. Add 'e' to these words and see how it changes them.

Write the changed word here.

Note how the sound of the vowel in the middle of the words changes.

gap + e →	
tap + e →	
fat + e →	
mat + e →	
rat + e →	
hop + e →	
mop + e →	
not + e →	
pip + e →	
rip + e →	

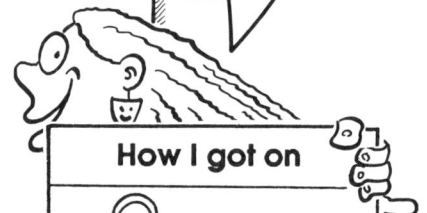

NOW Get someone to check your spellings. Turn over and try to write the words correctly several times without copying. Then get a partner to test you.

How I got on

Number of words correct

10
9 — Hot shot speller
8
7
6 — Need some more practice
5
4
3
2 — Need lots of practice
1
0

THE SPELLOMETER

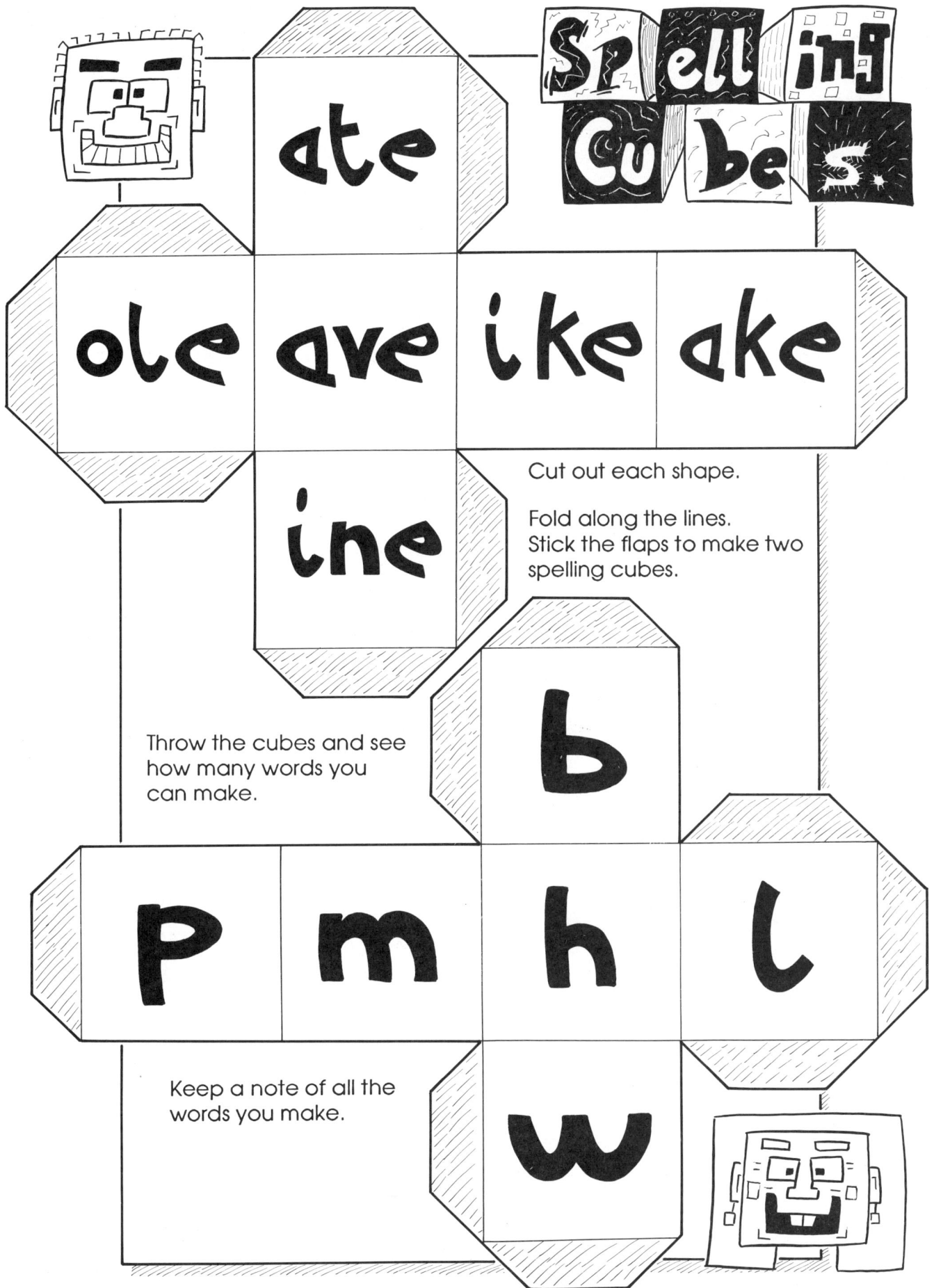

Spelling Cubes

ate

ole ave ike ake

ine

Cut out each shape.

Fold along the lines.
Stick the flaps to make two
spelling cubes.

b

Throw the cubes and see
how many words you
can make.

P m h l

w

Keep a note of all the
words you make.

KEY TO SPELLING

Say the word - does it sound right? Look at the word - does it look right?

FUN-AND-GAMES

Spelling needn't be boring or hard work! Sometimes it is fun to play with letter patterns!

Finish each 'word' off by adding the ending.
Some words are real words. Some are nonsense words.
Circle the real words you have made.
Write the real words in the boxes. Don't copy!

-ide

P_____   j_____   pr_____
sl_____   h_____   thr_____
br_____   w_____   c_____

-oke

P_____   sp_____   j_____
d_____   m_____   pl_____
scr_____   sm_____   ch_____

How I got on

Number of words correct	
10	Hot shot speller
9	
8	
7	Need some
6	more practice
5	
4	
3	Need lots of
2	practice
1	
0	

THE SPELLOMETER

NOW Get someone to check your spellings. Turn over and try to write the words correctly several times without copying. Then get a partner to test you.

Look for letter patterns in words.

THERMOMETER

CIRCLE THE LETTER PATTERN THAT YOU CAN SEE TWICE IN THIS WORD.

CHALLENGE!

Look carefully at the word on the board. Say it to yourself slowly. Cover it. Try to write it without copying!

Finish each of the words below. Write each word underneath without copying.

aft___

k__b

er → t__m

teach___

filt___

burn___

en__gy

int__esting ← **er**

obs__ve

diff__ent

How I got on

Number of words correct

10	Hot shot speller
9	
8	
7	
6	Need some more practice
5	
4	
3	
2	Need lots of practice
1	
0	

THE SPELLOMETER

NOW Get someone to check your spellings. Turn over and try to write the words correctly several times without copying. Then get a partner to test you.

SPELLING RULES O.K.?

Look out for the 'y' at the end of words.

IN MATHS THERE ARE NUMBER PATTERNS THAT HELP US.

$1 \times 10 = 10$
$2 \times 10 = 20$
$3 \times 10 = 30$
$4 \times 10 = ?$

Here is a spelling pattern to help you too.

If a word ends with a vowel + 'y'
● Just add 's' e.g. buy - buys

If a word ends with a consonant + 'y'
● Drop the 'y' and add 'ies' e.g., party - parties.

Use the pattern. Fill in the correct boxes.

word	+ 's'	-'y' + 'ies'
key		
fly		
city		
tray		
baby		
marry		
annoy		
hurry		
multiply		
guy		

How I got on

Number of words correct

10 9 8 — Hot shot speller

7 6 5 — Need some more practice

4 3 2 1 0 — Need lots of practice

THE SPELLOMETER

NOW Turn over. Get someone to check your spellings. Practise writing the 10 new words you have written without copying. Get a partner to test you.

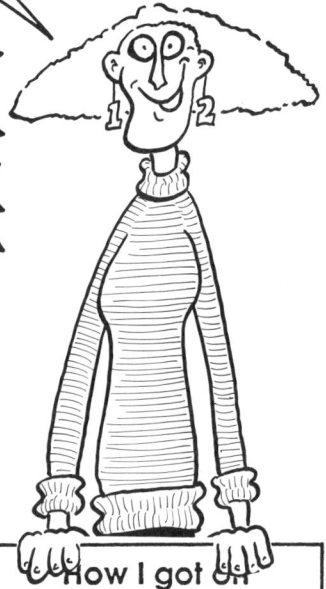

KEY TO SPELLING

INPUT AND OUTPUT MACHINE

We sometimes change the meaning of words by adding a suffix at the end.

INPUT

SPELLING OPERATION
+ FUL

OUTPUT

WORDS IN

WORDS OUT

USE

JOY

USEFUL

Feed these words into the machine.

Write what the words would be when they came out.

wonder	+	ful	▷
truth	+	ful	▷
hope	+	ful	▷
power	+	ful	▷
cheer	+	ful	▷

Now put these words through this machine.

taste		
care	INPUT	+ less	OUTPUT
use		
speech		
end		

How I got on

Number of words correct	
10	Hot shot speller
9	
8	
7	
6	Need some more practice
5	
4	
3	
2	Need lots of practice
1	
0	

THE SPELLOMETER

NOW

Get someone to check your spellings. Turn over and try to write the words correctly several times without copying. Then get a partner to test you.

Look for letter patterns in words.

WHAT'S COOKING ?

Finish icing these cakes with the correct letters and write the whole words as well.

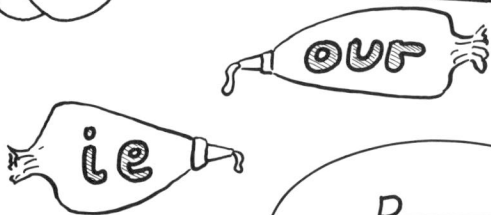

Can you spell the word 'ingredient'?

our

ie

p_____

p_____

p__ce

f____ld

col_____

flav_____

bel__ve

fr____nd

fl_____

h_____

How I got on

Number of words correct		
10		Hot shot speller
9		
8		
7		Need some
6		more practice
5		
4		
3		
2		Need lots of
1		practice
0		

THE SPELLOMETER

NOW

Get someone to check your spellings. Turn over and try to write the words correctly several times without copying. Then get a partner to test you.

A SPELL OF WEIGHT TRAINING

Are you strong enough to lift the weight to make all the 'ight' words?

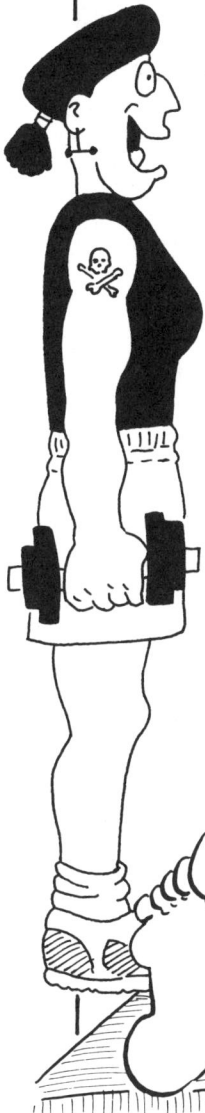

n [ ]
f [ ]
l [ ]
r [ ]
m [ ]

he [ ]
we [ ]
e [ ]
fr [ ]
br [ ]

ight   ight

Record your words here

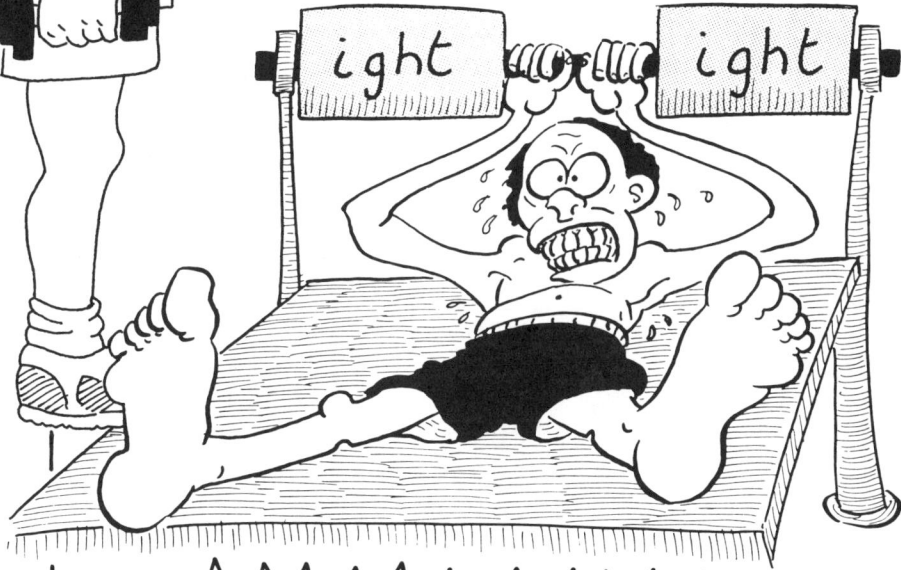

How I got on

Number of words correct

10
9
8   Hot shot speller
7
6
5   Need some more practice
4
3
2
1   Need lots of practice
0

THE SPELLOMETER

CHALLENGE!
Look carefully at this word **frightened**. Try to remember how to spell it without copying.

NOW
Get someone to check your spellings. Turn over. Practise spelling the 10 'ight' words above without copying. Get a partner to test you.

KEY TO SPELLING

FACE THE MUSIC!

Look out for soft 'c' and soft 'g' words.

Sometimes it helps spelling to look at and listen to the words.

- Say 'face the music' slowly.
- Listen to the sound of the 'c' in both words.
  - in 'fa**c**e' it is a soft 'c' and sounds like an 's'
  - in 'musi**c**' it is a harder 'c'

RULE:
Whenever 'c' is followed by a letter 'e' 'i' or 'y' it is said like an 's'.
Whenever 'g' is followed by a letter 'e' 'i' or 'y' it is said like an 'j'.

Look at the words.
Tick the ones containing a soft 'c' or soft 'g'.

dance

emergency

across

gentle

bag

city

age

traffic

nice

gone

face

energy

cat

rigid

again

strange

How I got on

Number of words correct	
10	Hot shot speller
9	
8	
7	Need some more practice
6	
5	
4	
3	
2	Need lots of practice
1	
0	

THE SPELLOMETER

NOW

Turn over and try to write the soft 'c' and soft 'g' words without copying.
Check your spelling. Practise writing the words several times, then get a partner to test you.

© 1992 Folens Ltd.   This page may be photocopied for classroom use only   Page 22

IN DAYS OF OLD

Read this passage from a History book. Fill in the words 'age' and 'old' in the gaps.

In days of _____ many people lived

in cott _____ s in small vill _____ s.

B_____ pirates set out on voy _____ s

in search of g_____ .

Here are some more words with 'old' or 'age' missing. Complete the words.

mess _____	s _____
s _____ ier	langu _____

Write all the 'old' words on this page here

Write all the 'age' words here.

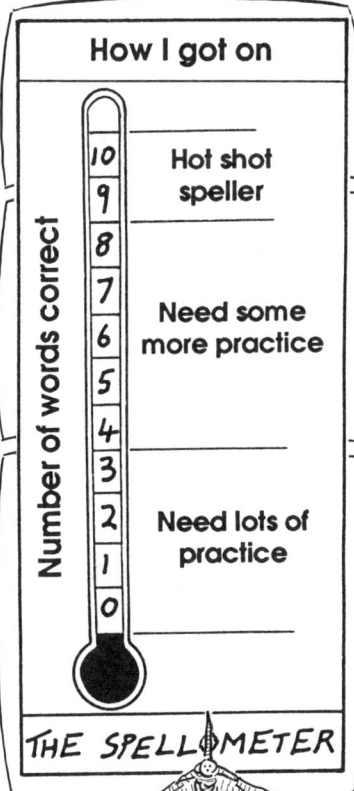

How I got on

Number of words correct	
10	Hot shot speller
9	
8	
7	Need some more practice
6	
5	
4	
3	
2	Need lots of practice
1	
0	

THE SPELLOMETER

NOW

Turn over and try to write the words correctly several times without copying. Then get a partner to test you.

Look out for words with silent letters.

SILENCE!

Can you spot the silent letters in the words below? Say the words. Circle the silent letters.

comb	
sign	
know	
knock	
talk	
wrong	
guitar	
guilty	
write	
climb	

Cover the words and write them again without copying.

How I got on

Number of words correct

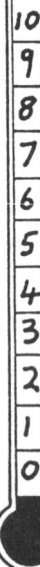

10
9 Hot shot speller
8
7
6 Need some more practice
5
4
3
2 Need lots of practice
1
0

THE SPELLOMETER

NOW Get someone to check your spellings. Turn over and try to write the words correctly several times without copying. Then get a partner to test you.

When a verb ends in 'e' we usually drop the 'e' when adding 'ing'.

FINISHING THE JOB PROPERLY!
PART 1

spell + ing = spelling

giv + e + ing = giving

With some verbs you can just add 'ing'.

When the verb ends with an 'e' we usually drop the 'e' then add 'ing'.

Fill in this chart correctly.

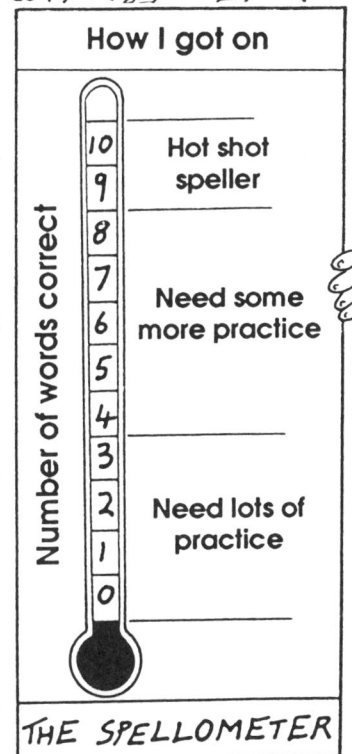

verb	add 'ing'	drop 'e' then add 'ing'
look		
use		
hope		
live		
go		
bite		
draw		
come		
write		
save		
fly		
fight		
smoke		
grumble		
handle		

How I got on

Number of words correct

10	Hot shot speller
9	
8	
7	Need some
6	more practice
5	
4	
3	
2	Need lots of
1	practice
0	

THE SPELLOMETER

NOW Get someone to check your spellings. Turn over. Practise spelling the 10 words in the third column without copying. Get a partner to test you.

FINISHING THE JOB PROPERLY ! PART 2

Look out for verbs that double the last letter before adding 'ed'.

wait + ed

waited

pat + t + ed

patted

With some verbs your can just add 'ed'.

When the next to last letter has a short vowel sound, you often double the last letter then add 'ed'.

Finish the chart correctly.

verb	add 'ed'	double the last letter then add 'ed'
fit		
end		
spot		
pop		
plant		
rob		
tap		
pin		
bat		
prod		
thank		
miss		
beg		
travel		
crack		

How I got on

THE SPELLOMETER

Number of words correct

10	Hot shot
9	speller
8	
7	
6	Need some
5	more practice
4	
3	
2	Need lots of
1	practice
0	

NOW

Get someone to check your spellings.
Turn over. Practise spelling the 10 words in the third column without copying. Get a partner to test you.

FINISHING THE JOB PROPERLY! PART 3

Watch out for verbs that end in 'y'.

With some verbs you can just add 'ed'.

When the verb ends in 'y' you drop the 'y' and add 'ied'.

Fill in the chart correctly.

verb	add 'ed'	drop the 'y' add 'ied'
bang		
try		
climb		
spy		
cry		
empty		
hurry		
carry		
lift		
jump		
marry		
reply		
supply		
multiply		
post		

How I got on

Number of words correct	
10	Hot shot speller
9	
8	
7	Need some more practice
6	
5	
4	
3	
2	Need lots of practice
1	
0	

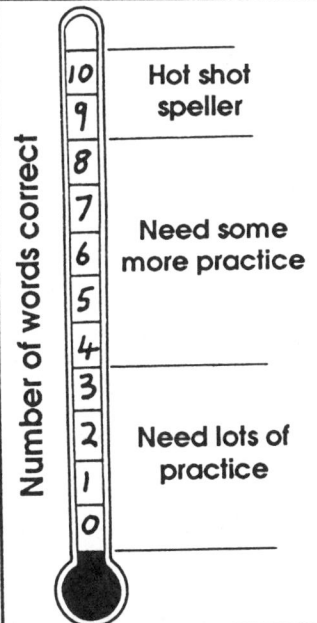

THE SPELLOMETER

NOW Get someone to check your spellings. Turn over. Practise spelling the 10 words in the third column without copying. Get a partner to test you.

KEY TO SPELLING

ROOTS

Look for 'root' words hiding in longer words.

TEACHER'S FAMILY TREE

TEACHER

MUM | DAD

MUM'S MUM | MUM'S DAD | DAD'S MUM | DAD'S DAD

Sometimes it helps to remember spellings if we can spot the 'root' word from which the word has grown:

re(turn)

(use)ful

dis(trust)

Look at these words. Circle the 'root' word in each.

disagree

raining

comfortable

performance

signal

careless

punishment

impossible

bakery

wonderful

How I got on

10	Hot shot speller
9	
8	
7	Need some more practice
6	
5	
4	
3	Need lots of practice
2	
1	
0	

Number of words correct

THE SPELLOMETER

NOW

Get someone to check your answers. Turn over and practise spelling the 10 root words you have spotted without copying. Get a partner to test you.

KEY TO SPELLING
Look carefully at differences in words to remember them.

ead

eat

eak

Dive in. Only pick up the words in each lane which contain the letter pattern on your starting block.

please

beat

healthy

east

leave

weak

leader

great

speak

ready

near

steam

real

seat

leaf

head

cheat

break

① ② ③

Deliver your words here.

How I got on

Number of words correct

10 Hot shot
9 speller
8
7 Need some
6 more practice
5
4
3
2 Need lots of
1 practice
0

THE SPELLOMETER

NOW

Get someone to check your spellings. Turn over and try to write the words correctly several times without copying. Then get a partner to test you.

Look for common letter patterns in words.

RAIN   SNOW   SUN

WE USE SYMBOLS WHEN WE STUDY THE WEATHER.

Below we use these symbols to help us with spelling.

- When you see [cloud] write the letter pattern 'ain',
- When you see [snowflake] write the letter pattern 'ow'
- When you see [sun] write the letter pattern 'un'

Write the whole word out each time too.

[sun] til

mount [cloud]   bel [snowflake]   ag [cloud]

sl [snowflake] ly   expl [cloud]   [sun] less

[sun] der   shad [snowflake]   Brit [cloud]

How I got on

Number of words correct	
10	Hot shot speller
9	
8	
7	Need some more practice
6	
5	
4	
3	
2	Need lots of practice
1	
0	

THE SPELLOMETER

NOW Get someone to check your spellings. Turn over and try to write the words correctly several times without copying. Then get a partner to test you.

KEY TO SPELLING

Group words according to common letter patterns

MOTORWAY MADNESS

Which words are allowed in each coned-off lane of the motorway?

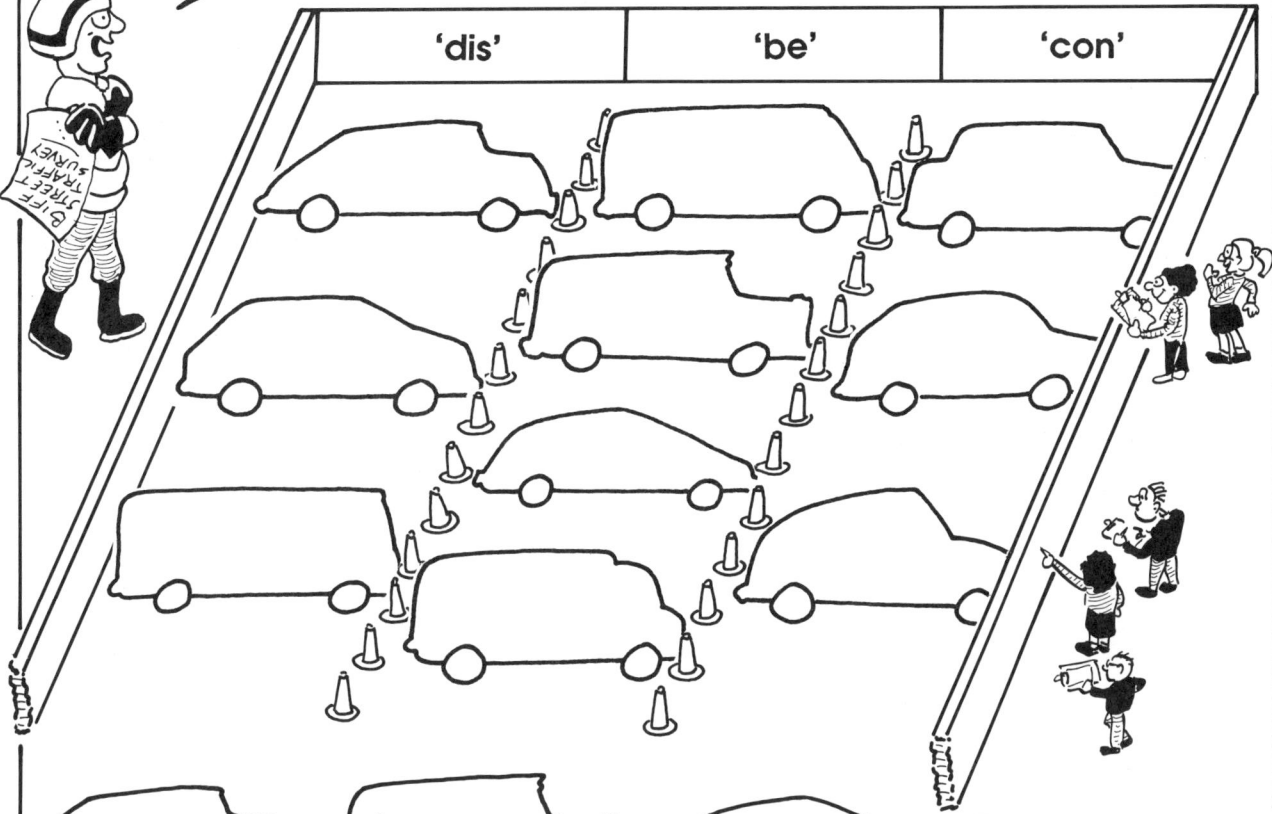

'dis'	'be'	'con'

STREET TRAFFIC SURVEY

discover

become

before

because

contain

contest

connect

discuss

disappear

beneath

How I got on

Number of words correct	
10	Hot shot speller
9	
8	
7	Need some more practice
6	
5	
4	
3	
2	Need lots of practice
1	
0	

THE SPELLOMETER

NOW

Get someone to check your spellings. Turn over and try to write the words correctly several times without copying. Then get a partner to test you.

ALPHABETICAL ORDER QUIZ – PART 1

KEY TO SPELLING
We need to use alphabetical order to help look up words in dictionaries.

Read the clues. Finish the words by choosing the endings from the bottom of the page.

Write the words in alphabetical order according to the second letter.

ALF

BOOTS

CURLY

DIPPY

ERIC

FRED

GAIL

HAPPY

1. Break into small pieces   sm _____
2. A fish with sharp teeth   sh _____
3. The bone of your head   sk _____
4. Shoes worn indoors   sl _____
5. Seat on a horse's back   sa _____
6. For digging with   sp _____
7. A four-sided shape   sq _____
8. Quiet   si _____
9. Frozen rain   sn _____
10. Wear it for warmth   sc _____

_____
_____
_____
_____
_____
_____
_____
_____
_____
_____

IONA   KATE   NELLIE   MOODY   OLLY   QUIZZY   RAY   TRACE   UNA

JANE   LARRY   PARROT   SID   VAL   WALLY

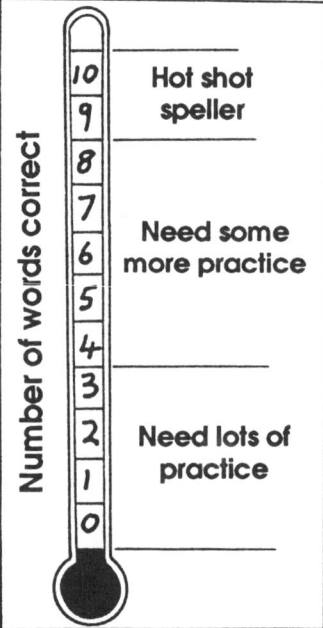

X-MAN   YUPPIE   ZORRO

_____ ddle	_____ arf	_____ ippers
_____ ull	_____ ash	_____ lent
_____ ow	_____ vare	_____ ark
	_____ ade	

How I got on

Number of words correct	
10	Hot shot speller
9	
8	
7	Need some more practice
6	
5	
4	
3	
2	Need lots of practice
1	
0	

THE SPELLOMETER

NOW
Get someone to check your spellings. Turn over and try to write the words correctly several times without copying. Then get a partner to test you.

KEY TO SPELLING

We need to use alphabetical order to help look up words in dictionaries.

ALF

Read the clues. Finish the words by choosing the endings from the bottom of the page.

Write the words in alphabetical order according to the third letter.

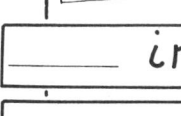

BOOTS

CURLY

DIPPY

ERIC

FRED

GAIL

HAPPY

1. To divide things up — sep_____

2. A soldier on guard — sen_____

3. Someone who serves you — ser_____

4. Winter is one — sea_____

5. More than two or three — sev_____

6. After the first — sec_____

7. You do this with a needle — sew_____

8. To grab hold — sei_____

9. A seat — set_____

10. Not thinking of others — sel_____

IONA · JANE · KATE · LARRY · MOODY · NELLIE · OLLY · PARROT · QUIZZY · RAY · SID · TRACE · UNA · VAL · WALLY · X-MAN · YUPPIE · ZORRO

____ing	____arate	____ond
____ze	____son	____try
____vant	____fish	____eral
____tee		

NOW

Get someone to check your spellings. Turn over. Practise writing the 10 new words you have written without copying. Get a partner to test you.

How I got on

Number of words correct

10
9 — Hot shot speller
8
7
6 — Need some more practice
5
4
3
2 — Need lots of practice
1
0

THE SPELLOMETER

KEY TO SPELLING

COLOUR BY SPELLING!

Try to group words according to common letter patterns.

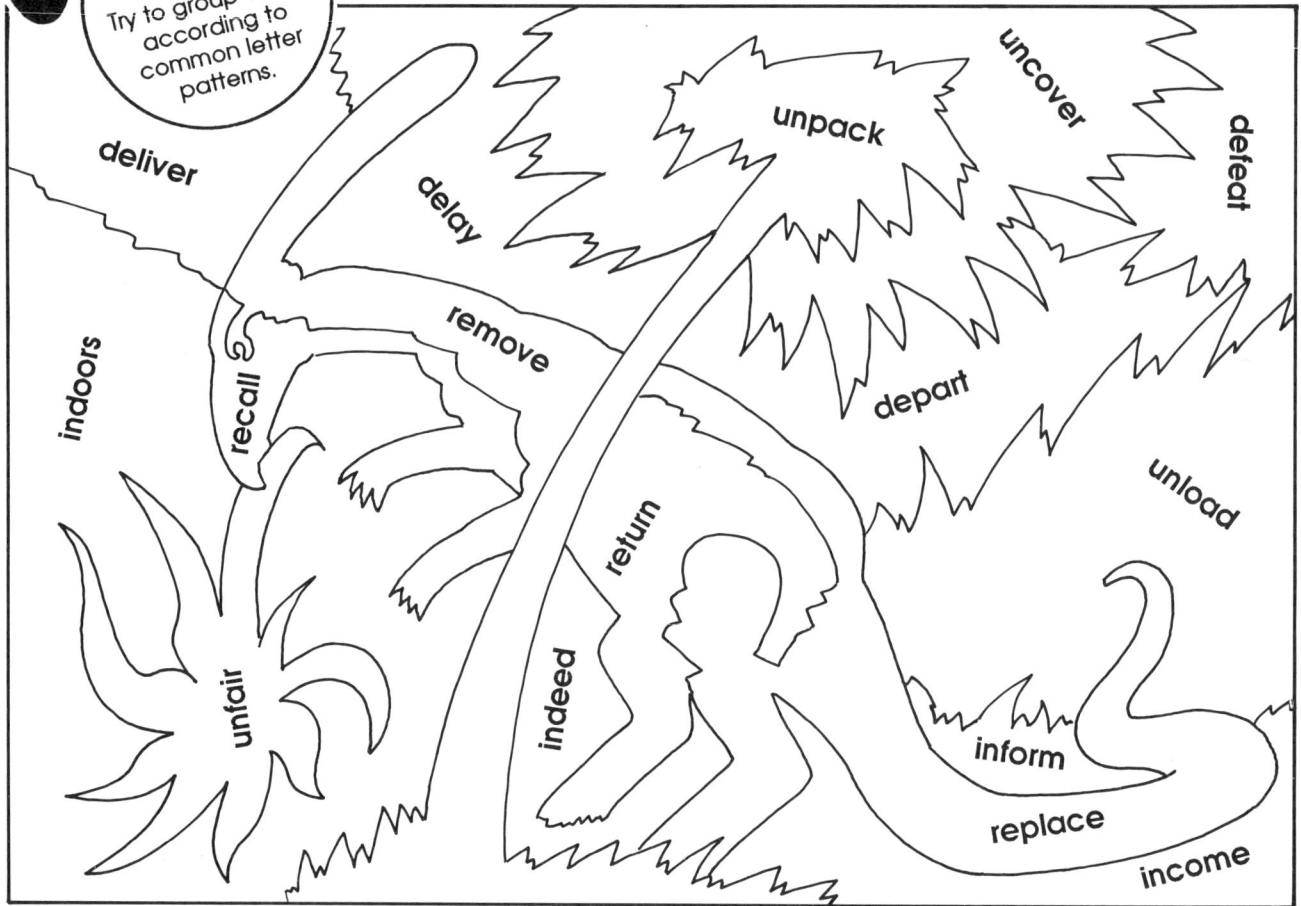

deliver

delay

unpack

uncover

defeat

indoors

recall

remove

depart

unload

return

unfair

indeed

inform

replace

income

Create a picture by colouring in the spelling patterns.

Colour the word blocks:

'un' words green
're' words brown
'in' words black
'de' words blue.

On the back of your paper draw 4 columns.
Write out the sets of words without copying.

NOW

Get someone to check your spellings.
Choose ten of the words. Practice
writing them without copying. Get a partner to test
you.

How I got on

Number of words correct

10
9
8
7
6
5
4
3
2
1
0

Hot shot
speller

Need some
more practice

Need lots of
practice

THE SPELLOMETER

SPELLING-ON-A-PLATE

Sometimes it helps to break words down into smaller parts.

LOOK. THE PLATES FIT TOGETHER.

pre tend

ARCHAEOLOGICAL CHALLENGE!

Put these plates together to make new words.

When you have finished, turn over and practise writing the new words without copying. Get a partner to test you.

be	part	
de	able	
con	cause	*because*
dis	fect	
en	sider	
ex	agine	
for	agree	
im	form	
per	pect	
in	give	

How I got on

Number of words correct

10 — Hot shot speller
9
8
7 — Need some
6 — more practice
5
4
3
2 — Need lots of
1 — practice
0

THE SPELLOMETER

KEY TO SPELLING

Sometimes it helps to break words down into syllables.

SOMETIMES IT HELPS TO BREAK THINGS UP!

OUCH!

OW!

LET GO!

In spelling it helps to break words down into smaller parts called syllables.

| dif | fer | ent |

different

| in | ter | est | ing |

interesting

CHALLENGE!
Try to write these two words without copying:
different   interesting

Join each beginning syllable to the correct ending syllable.

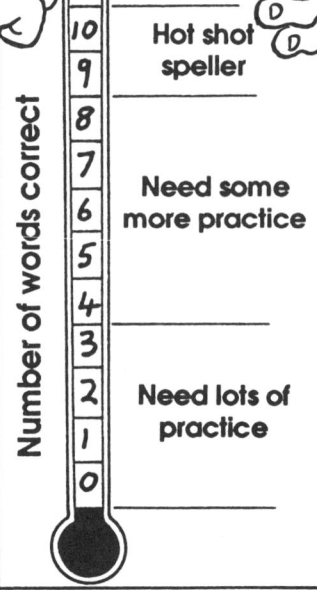

pro	ty	
my	time	
emp	vide	provide
some	cause	
moun	self	
be	ly	
bro	tain	
ex	ple	
lone	cuse	
peo	ken	

ow I got on

THE SPELLOMETER

Number of words correct

10
9 — Hot shot speller
8
7
6 — Need some more practice
5
4
3
2 — Need lots of practice
1
0

NOW

Get someone to check your spellings.
Turn over and try to write the words correctly several times without copying. Then get a partner to test you.

SPELLING CO-ORDINATES

Some words are made of two smaller words joined together.

	1	2	3	4	5	6
F	sea	over	any	room	my	rain
E	down	bow	foot	side	after	take
D	birth	class	stairs	step	under	when
C	some	self	ever	day	car	one
B	key	pet	thing	break	motor	is
A	fast	noon	ground	land	hole	way

Work out and make up the words from the co-ordinates given.

1. 3F + 6A =
2. 4B + 1A =
3. 5E + 2A =
4. 6D + 3C =
5. 2F + 6E =
6. 3E + 4D =
7. 5F + 2C =
8. 6B + 4A =
9. 1D + 4C =
10. 1F + 4E =

How I got on

Number of words correct

10	Hot shot speller
9	
8	
7	
6	Need some more practice
5	
4	
3	
2	Need lots of practice
1	
0	

THE SPELLOMETER

NOW

Get someone to check your spelling. Turn over and try to write the words correctly several times without copying. Then get a partner to test you.

LOOKING-FOR-PROOF-?

IT IS IMPORTANT TO READ WHAT YOU HAVE WRITTEN TO SEE IF YOU CAN SPOT ANY MISTAKES.

Read this story. There are 10 spelling mistakes in it. Find them and cross them out. Choose the correct spelling and write it over each mistake.

Correct words

quickly
wasn't
exciting
Wednesday
because
laughed
front
luckily
jumped
~~last~~

The Fright

Last

I was watching TV larst Wensday as usual. The programme wasent very exiting so I went for a walk. I walked quickley becos it was dark. Suddenly something jumpt out in frunt of me. Luckaly it was just a dog. I larfed!

How I got on

Number of words correct		
10	Hot shot
9	speller
8	
7	Need some
6	more practice
5	
4	
3	
2	Need lots of
1	practice
0	

THE SPELLOMETER

NOW Turn over. Practise writing the 10 correctly spelt words yourself without copying. Get a partner to test you.

DON'T-MENTION-IT!

Look at the letter patterns at the end of the words.

SORRY!

DON'T MENTION IT.

Finish the words below with either 'ment' or 'tion'. Then write the whole word again without copying.

pay_____	
ac_____	
na_____	
argu_____	
inven_____	
ques_____	
improve_____	
punish_____	
addi_____	
govern_____	

SCHOOL SAFETY OFFICER

How I got on

Number of words correct

10	Hot shot speller
9	
8	
7	Need some more practice
6	
5	
4	
3	Need lots of practice
2	
1	
0	

THE SPELLOMETER

NOW

Get someone to check your spellings. Turn over and try to write the words correctly several times without copying. Then get a partner to test you.

HOW DO YOU DO IT? PART 1

We can often just add 'ly' to adjectives to change them into adverbs.

HOW DID YOU DO IN THE TEST?

Adverbs
To make a word into an adverb we usually just add - ly

BADLY!

NEATLY!

AWFULLY!

BEAUTIFULLY!

Change these words into adverbs by adding 'ly'.

There are some that don't stick to this rule! Can you think of any?

| Write the adverbs |

sudden ——▷

love ——▷

quiet ——▷

careful ——▷

safe ——▷

painful ——▷

loud ——▷

neat ——▷

slow ——▷

cheerful ——▷

How I got on

Number of words correct

10	Hot shot speller
9	
8	
7	
6	Need some more practice
5	
4	
3	
2	Need lots of practice
1	
0	

THE SPELLOMETER

NOW

Get someone to check your spellings. Turn over and try to write the words correctly several times without copying. Then get a partner to test you.

HOW DO YOU DO IT? PART 2

HOW DID YOU DO?

Adverbs

*To make a word into an adverb - add 'ly'
BUT ...
If the word ends in 'le' - take away the 'le' then add 'ly'*

valuable - valuably

TERRIBLY!

REASONABLY!

HORRIBLY!

Finish the words with 'ible' or 'able'

Make them into adverbs.

poss_____ ⟶
valu_____ ⟶
reli_____ ⟶
terr_____ ⟶
horr_____ ⟶
comfort_____ ⟶
reason_____ ⟶
respons_____ ⟶
invis_____ ⟶
suit_____ ⟶

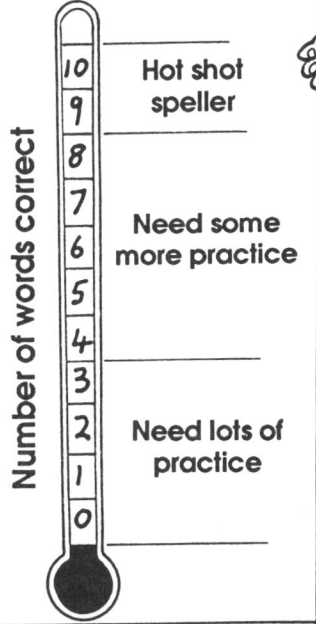

How I got on

Number of words correct	
10	Hot shot speller
9	
8	
7	Need some more practice
6	
5	
4	
3	
2	Need lots of practice
1	
0	

THE SPELLOMETER

NOW Get someone to check your spellings Turn over and try to write the words correctly several times without copying. Then get a partner to test you.

CONTRACTING and EXPANDING

Understanding the use of contraction helps spelling.

Sometimes we contract words when we write them. We use an apostrophe to show this.

I am ⟶ I'm   They are ⟶ they're

I couldn't do it.
I could not do it.

It wouldn't be nice.

Circle the contractions. Write each contraction in full underneath.

I'll soon be home.

I'm lovely!

I've got it.

It isn't fair.

You're first.

Don't do that!

I can't reach.

Quick. They're here.

I am	could not	they are	you are
I will	cannot	do not	I have
would not	is not		

How I got on

Number of words correct

10	Hot shot speller
9	
8	
7	Need some more practice
6	
5	
4	
3	Need lots of practice
2	
1	
0	

THE SPELLOMETER

NOW

Turn over. Practise writing the 10 contractions without copying. Get a partner to test you.

INSIDE-OUT !

- Take a letter from any of the outside circles.

- Add it to any of the five letter patterns in the shaded circles.

- Does it make a word?

- Experiment and see how many different words you can make in this way.

- Make a note of all the words you make.

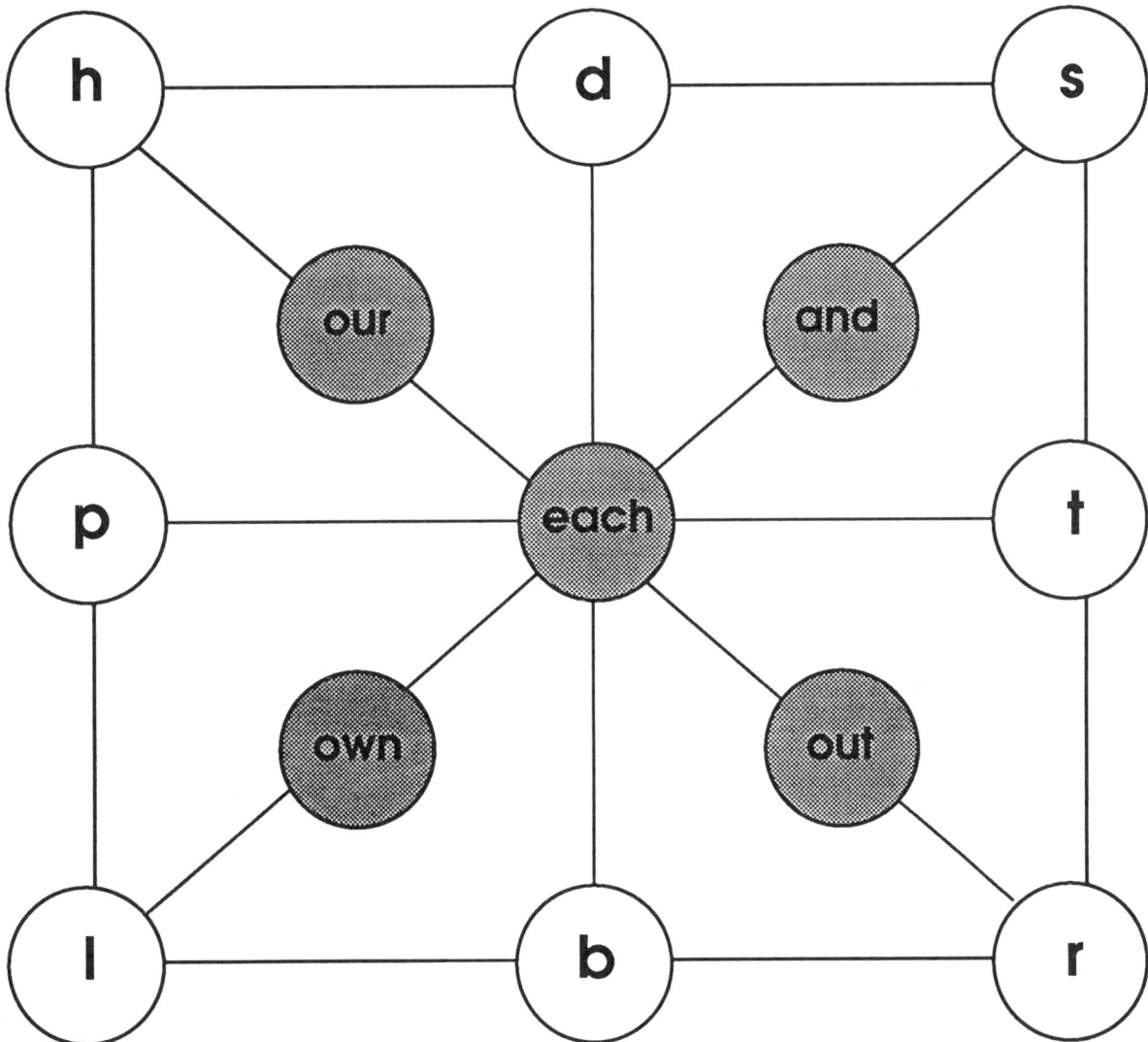

SPELLING SETS

KEY TO SPELLING

Don't be afraid to experiment with words.

WHAT WORDS COULD WE MAKE THAT BEGIN WITH THE LETTERS 'RE'?

CENT **RE**

$x = \frac{2}{3}$ $a + b$

READ   REMEMBER   RECORD

CHALLENGE!

Try to think of two new words that begin with the letters in the area where each of the sets below overlap.

Write your words

Use a dictionary to help you find some words, or to check your spellings, if you need to.

ang **le**

equ **al**

bot **tom**

diame **ter**

Leng **th**

NOW

Ask someone to check the spellings of your new words. Turn over and try to write the words correctly several times without copying. Then get a partner to test you.

H(..) got on

Number of words correct	
10	Hot shot
9	speller
8	
7	
6	Need some
5	more practice
4	
3	
2	Need lots of
1	practice
0	

THE SPELLOMETER

KEY TO SPELLING

Make up silly sentences to help you remember.

SILLY SPELLINGS

DON'T 'LET ON' THAT YOU SAW A SKELETON!

Minimum is a 'mini' mother

CHALLENGE!

Look carefully at the long words above. Say them slowly. Try to write them without copying.

Look at each of these words. On the other side of your paper try to make up a silly sentence about each one. Work with a partner if you can.

friend	expensive	boring	heard
nearly	lonely	scared	frightened
cupboard	outside		

NOW

Practise spelling the 10 words without copying. Get a partner to test you.

How I got on

Number of words correct

10 — Hot shot speller
9
8
7 — Need some more practice
6
5
4
3
2 — Need lots of practice
1
0

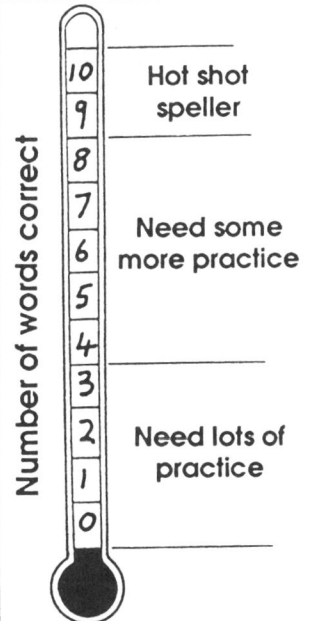

THE SPELLOMETER

IN-A-SPIN

- Stick the hexagon shapes on to card.

- Cut them out.

- Push a (cocktail) stick through the centre of each to make them into spinners.

- Spin them both and see how many different words you can make.

- Keep a note of all the words.

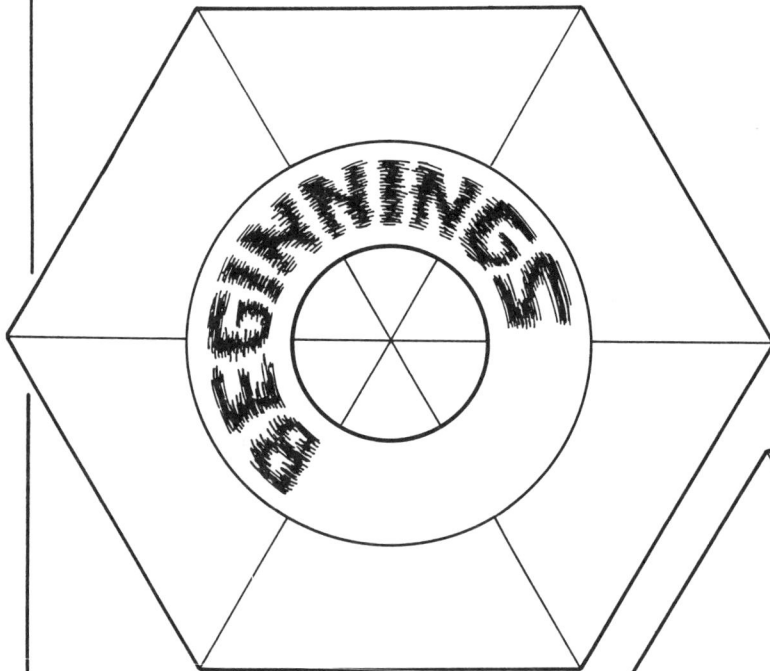

BEGINNINGS

ENDINGS

Spelling Cubes.

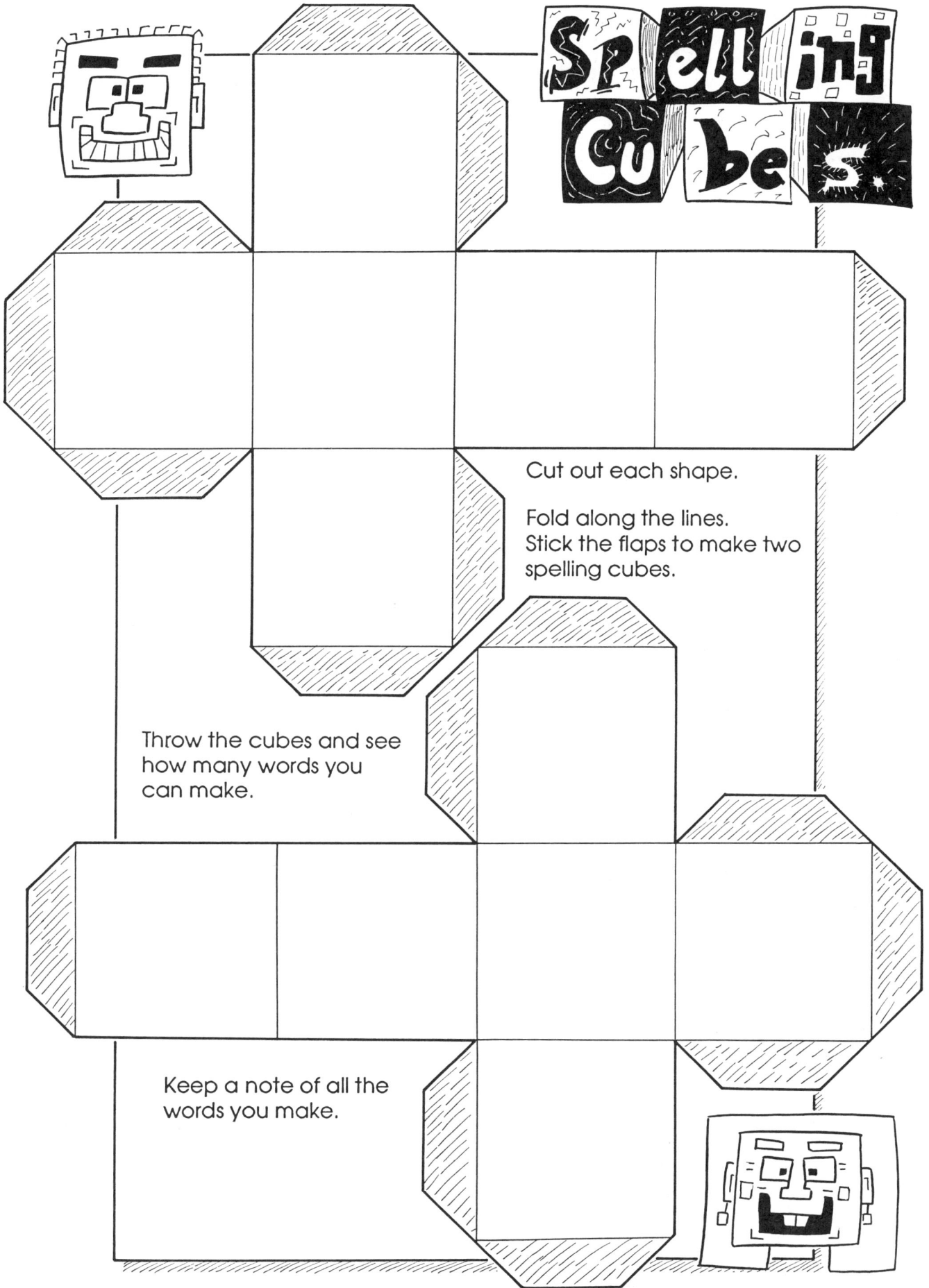

Cut out each shape.

Fold along the lines.
Stick the flaps to make two
spelling cubes.

Throw the cubes and see
how many words you
can make.

Keep a note of all the
words you make.

This page may be photocopied for classroom use only

My Spelling Hit List

Words I want to learn to spell:
(Ask your teacher to write them correctly for you.)

_____   _____   _____

_____   _____

Today's date: _____

Deadline for learning the Hit List: _____

(Fold) -

Spelling Hints

- Look carefully at each word you want to spell.
- Say it to yourself. See if the word looks the way it sounds.
- Look at the word and trace the word on your desk with your finger.
- Repeat this with your eyes closed.
- If a particular part of the word gives you difficulty underline or highlight it.
- Practise writing the tricky part of the word in your head.
- Shut your eyes. Try to see or spell the word in your head.
- Cover the word you want to spell.
- Write it from memory.
- Check your spelling with the teacher's spelling. If it is not correct try again.

Spelling the Hit List words: my attempt.

_____   _____   _____

_____   _____

Did you make the deadline: YES/NO   **How many did you get right** _____

5

Test yourself again 2 weeks from today on: _____

    This page may be photocopied for classroom use only